W9-CNR-948

Learning about Cats

THE AMERICAN SHORTHAIR CAT

by Joanne Mattern

Consultant:
Wayne Crabbs
Secretary
National American Shorthair Club

CAPSTONE
HIGH-INTEREST
BOOKS

an imprint of Capstone Press
Mankato, Minnesota

Capstone High-Interest Books are published by Capstone Press
151 Good Counsel Drive, P.O. Box 669, Mankato, Minnesota 56002
http://www.capstone-press.com

Copyright © 2003 by Capstone Press. All rights reserved.
No part of this publication may be reproduced in whole or in part, or stored in a retrieval
system, or transmitted in any form or by any means, electronic, mechanical,
photocopying, recording, or otherwise, without written permission of the publisher.
For information regarding permission, write to Capstone Press,
151 Good Counsel Drive, P.O. Box 669, Dept. R, Mankato, Minnesota 56002
Printed in the United States of America.

Library of Congress Cataloging-in-Publication Data
Mattern, Joanne, 1963–
    The American shorthair cat/by Joanne Mattern.
    p. cm.—(Learning about cats)
    Includes bibliographical references (p. 45) and index.
    Summary: Discusses the history, development, habits, and care of American
shorthair cats.
    ISBN 0-7368-1300-4 (hardcover)
    1. American shorthair cat—Juvenile literature. [1. American shorthair cat.
2. Cats. 3. Pets.] I. Title. II. Series.
SF449.A45 M28 2003
636.8'22—dc21   2001007744

Editorial Credits
Angela Kaelberer, editor; Karen Risch, product planning editor; Linda Clavel,
    series designer and illustrator; Gene Bentdahl, book designer; Jo Miller,
    photo researcher

Photo Credits
Chanan Photography, cover, 4, 6, 10, 13, 14, 16, 19, 20, 24, 26, 37, 38
Nancy M. McCallum, 9, 22, 28, 31, 32, 34
Photo by Mark McCullough, 40–41

1 2 3 4 5 6 07 06 05 04 03 02

Table of Contents

Quick Facts about the American Shorthair

Description

Size: American Shorthairs are medium- to large-sized cats.

Weight: A full-grown American Shorthair weighs between 8 and 15 pounds (3.6 and 6.8 kilograms).

Physical features: The American Shorthair has a muscular, sturdy body. Its coat is short and thick.

The American Shorthair has a wide head and round cheeks. Its nose is medium in length.

Color: American Shorthairs can be one of more than 80 colors and color patterns. Silver tabby is the most common color pattern. Other common colors and color patterns are brown tabby, red tabby, solid black, solid white, tortoiseshell, calico, and bi-color.

Development
Place of origin: The American Shorthair breed began in the United States. It is one of the oldest breeds in North America.

History of breed: The American Shorthair descended from cats that came to North America with European settlers more than 400 years ago. The breed once was called the Domestic Shorthair.

Numbers: In 2001, the Cat Fanciers' Association (CFA) registered 968 American Shorthair cats. Owners who register their American Shorthairs list the cats' breeding records with an official club. The CFA is the largest organization of cat breeders in North America.

Chapter 1

The American Shorthair Cat

The American Shorthair is one of North America's oldest cat breeds. American Shorthairs usually have calm, affectionate personalities and make good family pets. The cats also tend to be healthy and rarely need special care. These qualities make the breed one of the most popular in North America.

Appearance

Male American Shorthairs usually weigh between 11 and 15 pounds (5 and 6.8 kilograms). Females are smaller. They usually weigh between 8 and 12 pounds (3.6 and 5.4 kilograms).

Most cat breeds are fully grown at one year. But American Shorthairs may not reach their full size until they are three or four years old.

The American Shorthair is one of the most popular breeds in North America.

American Shorthairs have short, evenly thick fur. The fur feels hard to the touch.

Personality

American Shorthairs make good family pets. They get along well with children and seem to enjoy playing with them. American Shorthairs also get along well with dogs and other cats. They do not seem to enjoy being alone. For this reason, many Amcrican Shorthair owners who are not at home during the day own two or more cats.

American Shorthairs are affectionate and friendly. They often follow their owners from room to room. They may sit near their owners for hours.

The American Shorthair is a playful breed. They often play with cat toys. They also chase balls or crumpled pieces of paper. Some cat breeds are playful only as kittens. But American Shorthairs remain playful throughout their lives.

American Shorthairs are intelligent. Many of these cats seem to understand a

The American Shorthair is a playful breed.

number of human words. Owners often can train their American Shorthairs to come when called or fetch toys or other objects.

The American Shorthair is a quiet breed. The cats seldom meow unless they are hungry. Their meow is soft and low.

Chapter 2

Development of the Breed

The American Shorthair is one of the few cat breeds that developed in North America. Shorthaired cats came to North America with early explorers and settlers from Europe. The cats caught rats and mice on the ships.

Many historians believe the Pilgrims brought cats aboard the *Mayflower*. The American Shorthair breed descended from these early North American cats. A longhaired breed also can be traced back to these cats. This breed is called the Maine Coon.

A New Breed

People in North America kept the shorthaired cats to rid their houses and barns of rats and mice. In the late 1800s, North Americans

The American Shorthair developed in North America.

became interested in breeding and showing cats. People began bringing cats to North America from Europe and Asia. These cats sometimes were allowed to run free and mate with the native shorthaired cats. The resulting kittens often looked much different from the native shorthaired cats.

Some people wanted to preserve the native shorthaired breed. These people chose shorthaired cats with good qualities and began to breed them. They called the breed the Shorthair. Later, the breed's name was changed to the Domestic Shorthair.

The first Shorthair registered and shown in the United States was actually from Great Britain. This red male tabby was named Belle of Bradford. He was registered in 1901. The first registered Shorthair born in the United States was Buster Brown in 1904.

Gaining Respect

The Cat Fanciers' Association (CFA) was founded in 1906. The CFA recognized the Domestic Shorthair as one of the first five

The first Shorthair registered in the United States was a red tabby that may have looked like this cat.

pedigreed cat breeds. This recognition meant that Domestic Shorthairs could compete in cat shows.

For many years, the Domestic Shorthair received little respect and attention from cat show judges and breeders. These people preferred breeds from other countries. These breeds included the Persian and the Siamese.

Domestic Shorthairs could compete only in the household pets class at many cat shows. Cat clubs often did not even provide cages or trophies for Domestic Shorthairs at cat shows.

The Domestic Shorthair breed began to gain respect during the 1960s. In 1964, a silver tabby male named Shawnee Sixth Son won the CFA's Kitten of the Year award. Nikki Horner was Sixth Son's owner. In 1965, Horner won another honor. Her silver tabby Shawnee Trademark was named CFA's Cat of the Year.

In 1966, breeders voted to change the breed's name from Domestic Shorthair to American Shorthair. The name was changed to reflect this breed's history as a truly American cat.

Silver tabbies similar to this cat were the first Domestic Shorthair CFA Champions.

Chapter 3

Today's American Shorthair

Today, the American Shorthair is one of the most popular cat breeds in North America. The cats' friendly, playful personalities make them good family pets.

Color Patterns

American Shorthairs' coats can be one of more than 80 combinations of colors and patterns. Some of these cats are one solid color. Others have patches and markings of two or more colors. These colors include white, black, blue, red, cream, and silver. Blue is a shade of gray. Red and cream are shades of orange.

Silver tabby is the most common American Shorthair color pattern. These cats have silver coats with black, striped markings. On their

Silver tabby is the most common American Shorthair color pattern.

foreheads, they have a black marking that looks like the letter "M."

Red tabby is another common color pattern among American Shorthairs. These cats have medium-orange fur with darker orange tabby markings.

Bi-color, smoke, and van patterns also are found in American Shorthairs. Bi-colors have patches of white and a solid color. Smoke cats have a white undercoat with an overcoat of another solid color. Vans have white coats with patches of another color on their head, tail, and legs.

American Shorthairs also may be tortoiseshell or calico. Calico cats' coats have large patches of three colors. The most common colors are white and shades of black and red. Tortoiseshells' coats are a mixture of red and black fur.

The red tabby, calico, and tortoiseshell patterns are linked to the cat's sex. A cat's color is determined by genes. These parts of cells are passed from parents to their offspring.

Calico American Shorthairs' coats have large patches of three colors.

An American Shorthair cat that meets the breed standard has a solid, powerful, and muscular body.

   Both female and male cats can carry a dominant gene for the red color. If the cat is male, it will almost always be a red tabby. If it is female, it will almost always be either a calico or a tortoiseshell.

Breed Standard

Today, many American Shorthairs compete in cat shows. Judges look for certain physical features when they judge an American Shorthair in a cat show. These features are called the breed standard.

An American Shorthair cat that meets the breed standard has a solid, powerful, and muscular body. The shoulders and chest are well-developed. The legs are long, straight, and muscular. The tail is medium to long. It is heavier at the base and thinner at the tip. An American Shorthair's coat should be short, thick, and even. The fur should feel hard to the touch.

An ideal American Shorthair has a large head with full cheeks. The large, wide eyes should be almond-shaped at the top and rounded at the bottom. The American Shorthair's ears should be medium-sized and slightly rounded at the tips. The cat's nose should be medium in length.

Chapter 4

Owning an American Shorthair

People who want an American Shorthair cat have several choices. Some people buy American Shorthairs from breeders. Others adopt cats from animal shelters or breed rescue organizations.

Breeders

People who want to show or breed an American Shorthair should buy one from a good breeder. These breeders make sure their cats are healthy and meet the breed standard. A breeder usually owns one or both of the kitten's parents. People who meet a kitten's mother or father can learn how the kitten might look and behave when it is grown.

Quality American Shorthair kittens are available from good breeders.

Cat shows are good places to meet American Shorthair breeders and see their cats.

Many American Shorthair breeders live in the United States and Canada. People often contact breeders at cat shows. Cat shows are good places to meet breeders, talk to them, and see their cats.

Buyers should check a breeder's references before buying a cat. Buyers should talk to other people who have bought cats from the breeder. Breeders also should provide buyers with the cat's medical history.

Animal Shelters

Animal shelters keep unwanted pets and try to find homes for them. A shelter can be an inexpensive place to adopt a cat.

Many people adopt pets from shelters so they can save animals' lives. Many more animals are brought to shelters than there are people available to adopt them. Animals that are not adopted often are euthanized. Shelter workers euthanize animals by injecting them with substances that stop their breathing or heartbeat.

Animal shelter adoptions are not a good choice for owners who want to show or breed their American Shorthairs. Cats adopted from shelters rarely have registration papers that list the animal's parents and breeder. Cats without these papers can only compete in the household pets category at cat shows.

People who adopt shelter cats may have another problem. Shelter workers may know little about the cats' parents, health, or behavior. Some of these cats may have problems with their health or behavior.

Rescue organizations may have registered American Shorthairs available.

Despite these problems, many good pets are available at animal shelters. Shelter adoptions are a good choice for people who do not want to breed or show their American Shorthairs.

Breed Rescue Organizations
People interested in adopting an American Shorthair may want to contact a breed rescue

organization. Rescue organizations find unwanted or neglected pets. They care for the pets and try to find new owners for them.

Rescue organizations are similar to animal shelters. But rescue organizations usually accept cats from only one or two breeds. Most rescue organizations do not euthanize cats. The organizations keep the cats until people are available to adopt them.

People may prefer to adopt an American Shorthair from a rescue organization for several reasons. Most rescue organizations are less expensive than breeders. Rescue organizations may have registered American Shorthairs available.

People can learn about rescue organizations in several ways. These organizations often have Internet sites. They also may advertise in magazines or newspapers. Animal shelter workers also may refer people to rescue organizations.

Chapter 5

Caring for an American Shorthair

The American Shorthair is a strong, healthy breed. With good care, these cats often live 15 to 20 years. People who adopt an American Shorthair should be ready for a long-term commitment to their cat.

Indoor and Outdoor Cats

Owners can help American Shorthairs live longer lives by keeping the cats inside. Cats that roam outdoors often catch serious diseases from other cats. Outdoor cats may be injured by cars or other animals.

Both indoor and outdoor cats may mark their territories by leaving their scent on objects they scratch. Cats also scratch to release tension and to keep their claws sharp.

Cats may mark their territories by leaving their scent on objects they scratch.

Owners should provide their American Shorthairs with a scratching post. Most cats will learn to scratch the post instead of the furniture, carpet, or curtains. Owners can buy a scratching post at a pet store or make one from wood and carpet.

Owners who keep their American Shorthairs inside must provide the cats with a litter box. These boxes are filled with small bits of clay or other material called litter.

Cats use litter boxes to eliminate waste. Owners should clean the waste out of the box each day. They should change the litter at least once each week. Cats may refuse to use a dirty litter box.

Feeding

Like all cats, American Shorthairs need high-quality food to stay healthy and strong. Most cat foods sold in supermarkets or pet stores provide a balanced, healthy diet.

Some owners feed their cats dry food. This food usually is less expensive than other types

Indoor American Shorthairs need a litter box.

of food. Dry food can help keep cats' teeth
clean. It does not spoil if it is left in a dish.

Other owners feed their cats moist, canned
food. This type of food can spoil easily. It
should not be left out for more than one hour.
Owners who feed their cats moist food usually
feed them twice each day. The amount of food
a cat needs depends on its size and appetite.

Owners should begin trimming their American Shorthairs' nails when the cats are young.

Cats need water to stay healthy. Owners should make sure their cats' bowls always are filled with fresh, clean water. The water should be changed at least once each day.

Grooming

American Shorthairs need little grooming. Owners should brush their American Shorthairs at least once each week with a soft bristle brush. Brushing removes loose hair. After brushing, owners should use a coarse comb to smooth out the cat's fur.

Owners should be careful when they are brushing and combing their American Shorthairs. Brushing and combing too hard can break off pieces of fur. It also can scrape the cat's skin.

Nail Care

The tip of a cat's claw is called the nail. Like other cats, American Shorthairs should have their nails trimmed every few weeks. This practice helps reduce damage if cats scratch the carpet or furniture.

Trimming also protects cats from ingrown nails. Ingrown nails can occur when a cat does not sharpen its claws often. The claws then grow into the bottom of the paw. This growth can cause painful infections of the paw.

Owners should begin trimming their American Shorthairs' nails when the cats are young. The kittens become used to having their

Owners should try to prevent American Shorthairs from overeating.

nails trimmed as they grow older. Veterinarians can show owners how to trim their cats' nails with a special nail clipper.

Dental Care

All cats need regular dental care to protect their teeth and gums from plaque. This coating of bacteria and saliva causes tooth decay and gum disease. Dry cat food helps remove plaque from American Shorthairs' teeth. Owners also should brush their American Shorthairs' teeth at least once each week. They can use a toothbrush made for cats or a soft cloth. Owners should use a toothpaste made for cats to brush the cats' teeth. Toothpaste made for people can make cats sick.

As American Shorthairs grow older, brushing may not be enough to remove the plaque from their teeth. These cats may need a veterinarian to clean their teeth once each year.

Health Problems

Most American Shorthairs have few health problems. But some American Shorthairs tend to overeat.

Owners must be careful that their American Shorthairs do not gain too much weight. Overweight cats are at a greater risk for health problems such as diabetes. This serious disease is caused when the cat's body does not produce a substance called insulin. The cat's body cannot store sugar or convert it to energy. Cats that have diabetes will die unless they receive regular shots of insulin.

Cats sometimes get inherited diseases. These diseases are passed down from adult cats to their kittens. Responsible cat breeders test their animals for inherited diseases. They do not breed animals that have these diseases.

Veterinarian Visits

American Shorthairs should visit a veterinarian at least once each year. Older cats may need to visit a veterinarian more often. Older cats are more likely to develop health problems than younger cats are. More frequent checkups help the veterinarian discover and treat these problems.

An owner who adopts an American Shorthair should take it to a veterinarian for a checkup right away. The veterinarian will check the cat's heart, lungs, and other organs. The veterinarian also will check the cat's eyes, ears, mouth, and coat.

The veterinarian also will give the American Shorthair several vaccinations. These shots of medicine help prevent serious diseases. These diseases include rabies, feline panleukopenia, and feline leukemia. Cats also

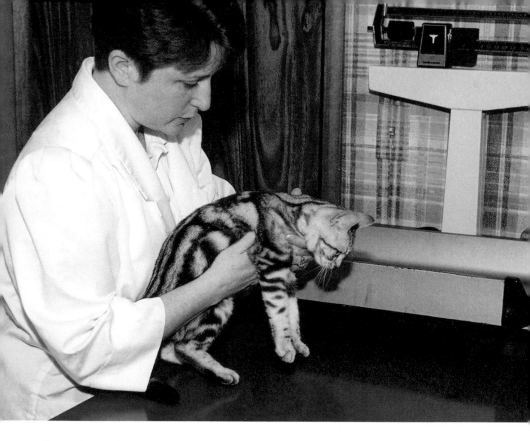

American Shorthairs should visit a veterinarian at least once each year.

can be vaccinated against several diseases that cause breathing problems.

Rabies is a deadly disease that is spread by animal bites. Both people and animals can die from rabies. Most states and provinces have laws that require owners to vaccinate their cats against rabies.

American Shorthairs make friendly, loving family companions.

Feline panleukopenia also is called feline distemper. This virus causes fever, vomiting, and death.

Feline leukemia attacks a cat's immune system. The cat cannot fight off infections and other illnesses. This disease is spread when a cat comes in contact with bodily fluids from an infected cat. Owners who show their American Shorthairs often vaccinate the cats against feline leukemia.

Owners should keep a record of the dates their American Shorthairs receive vaccinations. This record helps owners be sure their American Shorthairs have received all the vaccinations they need.

Spaying and Neutering

Veterinarians also spay and neuter cats. These surgeries remove a cat's reproductive organs and make it impossible for it to breed.

Owners who do not plan to breed their American Shorthairs should have them spayed or neutered. These surgeries prevent the birth of unwanted kittens. They also keep cats healthy by helping prevent diseases such as infections and cancers of the reproductive organs.

Spayed and neutered cats have calmer personalities than cats that are not spayed or neutered. They also are less likely to wander away from their homes.

The American Shorthair is a sturdy, healthy breed. This truly American cat can be a friendly, loving companion for the whole family.

BROWN TABBY
AMERICAN SHORTHAIR

Tabby markings

Rounded ears

Round, wide eyes

Straight, muscular legs

Quick Facts about Cats

A male cat is called a tom. A female cat is called a queen. A young cat is called a kitten. A family of kittens born at one time is called a litter.

Origin: Shorthaired cat breeds descended from a type of African wildcat called *Felis lybica*. Longhaired breeds may have descended from Asian wildcats. People domesticated or tamed these breeds as early as 1500 B.C.

Types: The Cat Fanciers' Association accepts 40 domestic cat breeds for competition. The smallest breeds weigh about 5 to 7 pounds (2.3 to 3.2 kilograms) when grown. The largest breeds can weigh more than 18 pounds (8.2 kilograms). Cat breeds may be either shorthaired or longhaired. Cats' coats can be a variety of colors. These colors include many shades of white, black, gray, brown, and red.

Reproduction: Most cats are sexually mature at 5 or 6 months. A sexually mature female cat goes into estrus several times each year. Estrus also is called "heat." During this time, she can mate with a male. Kittens are born about 65 days after breeding. An average litter includes four kittens.

Development: Kittens are born blind and deaf. Their eyes open about 10 days after birth. Their hearing develops at the same time. They can live on their own when they are 6 weeks old.

Life span: With good care, cats can live 15 or more years.

Sight: A cat's eyesight is adapted for hunting. Cats are good judges of distance. They see movement more easily than detail. Cats also have excellent night vision.

Hearing: Cats can hear sounds that are too high for humans to hear. A cat can turn its ears to focus on different sounds.

Smell: A cat has an excellent sense of smell. Cats use scents to establish their territories. Cats scratch or rub the sides of their faces against objects. These actions release a scent from glands between their toes or in their skin.

Taste: Cats cannot taste as many foods as people can. For example, cats are not very sensitive to sweet tastes.

Touch: Cats' whiskers are sensitive to touch. Cats use their whiskers to touch objects and sense changes in their surroundings.

Balance: Cats have an excellent sense of balance. They use their tails to help keep their balance. Cats can walk on narrow objects without falling. They usually can right themselves and land on their feet during falls from short distances.

Communication: Cats use many sounds to communicate with people and other animals. They may meow when hungry or hiss when afraid. Cats also purr. Scientists do not know exactly what causes cats to make this sound. Cats often purr when they are relaxed. But they also may purr when they are sick or in pain.

Words to Know

calico (KAL-i-koh)—a cat that has patches of red, white, and black fur

diabetes (dye-uh-BEE-teez)—a disease that occurs when a person or animal's body does not produce a substance called insulin

estrus (ESS-truss)—a physical state of a female cat during which she will mate with a male cat; estrus also is known as "heat."

euthanize (YOO-thuh-nize)—to put an animal to death by injecting it with a substance that stops its breathing or heartbeat

neuter (NOO-tur)—to remove a male animal's testicles so it cannot reproduce

spay (SPAY)—to remove a female animal's uterus and ovaries so it cannot reproduce

tortoiseshell (TOR-tuh-shell)—a cat that has a mixture of red and black fur

vaccination (vak-suh-NAY-shun)—a shot of medicine that protects a person or animal from disease

To Learn More

Commings, Karen. *Guide to Owning an American Shorthair.* Popular Cat Library. Philadelphia: Chelsea House, 1999.

Davis, Karen Leigh. *American Shorthair Cats: Everything about Purchase, Care, Nutrition, Health Care, Behavior, and Showing.* A Complete Pet Owner's Manual. Hauppauge, N.Y.: Barron's, 1999.

Fogle, Bruce. *The New Encyclopedia of the Cat.* New York: DK Publishing, 2001.

Quasha, Jennifer. *Shorthaired Cats in America.* A Kid's Cat Library. New York: PowerKids Press, 2000.

You can read articles about American Shorthairs in *Cat Fancy* magazine.

Useful Addresses

American Cat Fanciers Association (ACFA)
P.O. Box 1949
Nixa, MO 65714-1949

Canadian Cat Association (CCA)
289 Rutherford Road South
Unit 18
Brampton, ON L6W 3R9
Canada

Cat Fanciers' Association (CFA)
P.O. Box 1005
Manasquan, NJ 08736-0805

The International Cat Association (TICA)
P.O. Box 2684
Harlingen, TX 78551

Internet Sites

American Cat Fanciers Association
http://www.acfacat.com

American Veterinary Medical Association
Presents: Care for Pets
http://www.avma.org/care4pets

Canadian Cat Association
http://www.cca-afc.com

Cat Fanciers' Association
http://www.cfainc.org

Cats Central
http://www.cats-central.com

Fanciers Breeder Referral List—American
Shorthair
http://www.breedlist.com/
american-sh-breeders.html

Index

animal shelter, 23, 25–26, 27

Belle of Bradford, 12
breeder, 13, 15, 23–24, 25, 27, 36
breed rescue organization, 23, 26–27
breed standard, 21, 23
Buster Brown, 12

Cat Fanciers' Association, 12, 15
cat show, 12, 13, 15, 21, 23, 24, 25, 26, 38
claw, 29, 33
coat, 17, 18, 21, 36
color, 17–18, 20
   bi-color, 18
   calico, 18, 20
   smoke, 18
   solid, 17, 18
   tabby, 12, 15, 17–18, 20
   tortoiseshell, 18, 20
   van, 18

dental care, 31, 34–35
disease, 29, 34, 35–38, 39
Domestic Shorthair, 12–13, 15

food, 30–31, 34

grooming, 32–33

nail care, 33–34
neuter, 39

personality, 7, 8, 17, 39

registration papers, 25

Shawnee Sixth Son, 15
Shawnee Trademark, 15
spay, 39

vaccination, 36–39
veterinarian, 34, 35, 36, 39